Among the Absent

New and Selected Poems

by

Neva Herrington

Finishing Line Press
Georgetown, Kentucky

Among the Absent

New and Selected Poems

ISBN 978-1-63534-967-2 First Edition

ACKNOWLEDGMENTS

Blue Stone & Other Poems (Dallas: Still Point Press, 1986)
Her BMW and Other Poems (Columbus: Pudding House Publications, 2007)
Open Season (Cincinnati: David Robert Books, 2015)

Blue Stone & Other Poems was a Pushcart Foundation selection for "Writer's Choice," 1986.

The author expresses her appreciation to the editors of the following publications in which some of these poems first appeared: *Ascent*, "Lilacs," "The Drinker's Christmas"; *The Chariton Review,* "A Postcard from Spain," "Not Quite Loneliness in Texas," "The Size of Childhood," "Visit to Jan in Open Season," "Woodchuck at the Art Colony"; *The Comstock Review,* "Pumpkin Judging"; *Confrontation,* "Her BMW"; *Connecticut River Review,* "Courtship," "Facing Fort Trumbull with Charles," "Old, My Father Invented a Machine"; *Inlet*, "Daughter in Texas," "If You Were a Character in Chekhov," "Grandmother Singing"; *Nimrod*, "Dining with Marjorie"; *Southwest Review,* "Blue Stone," "Bakery Sonnet," "Rat Poem"; *The Southern Review,* "Original"; *Wind*, "Overnight," "The Father Maker"

"Original" appeared in the 1984 edition of *Anthology of Magazine Verse and Yearbook of American Poetry* (Monitor Books), "The Bakery Sonnet" in its 1985 edition. "Not Quite Loneliness in Texas" is anthologized in Roth Publishing's Poem Finder. "Woodchuck at the Art Colony" is published in *Entering the Free World* (Amherst: Waverly Press, 2011), an anthology of poems by Fellows at the Virginia Center for the Creative Arts.

The poem "Blue Stone" won *Southwest Review's* first Stover Award.

Grateful Acknowledgment is made to the Corporation of Yaddo and to the Virginia Center for the Creative Arts for residencies during which some of the these poems were written.

Publisher: Leah Maines
Editor: Christen Kincaid
Cover Art: Mary Page Evans
Author Photo: Angela Neal
Cover Design: Elizabeth Maines McCleavy

Printed in the USA on acid-free paper.
Order online: www.finishinglinepress.com
            also available on amazon.com

Author inquiries and mail orders:
Finishing Line Press
P. O. Box 1626
Georgetown, Kentucky 40324
U. S. A.

Table of Contents

From *Open Season* (2015)

New Poems

For Rodger

From

Blue Stone and Other Poems (1986)

If You Were a Character in Chekhov

If you were a character in Chekhov,
You would be the one to say, "I will tear
Love out of my heart by the roots." As if

Anyone can. What can I do for you?
Drink, take pills, marry the wrong one, at some
Unpracticed moment you will know the lines

That are yourself. There's also the girl
Who in the last act will say it's good luck
To love even the one turning away,

Knowing love isn't a root or a part
But the light locating you in the dark
Performance. Love is out of your hands.

Blue Stone

The worst tourist in Scotland takes
scenes as they come, treads down castles,
hears monuments explained from a bus,
rides through a town of empty streets

always deserted, the driver says,
like towns in American Westerns,
on foot to a famous height sinks
in burrs and mud, creeps damp stones

to a dungeon latrine, marches on jewels,
rooms of prayers and blood, leaves
the film in the camera so long
only a miracle could keep it true,

remembers finally the blue stone
on the northern beach, flat as a table,
true to its one color, some
solitary plot of its own.

Original

Those woods are a space now,
a fixed outline, a painting
you spoil every day,

trying to make the seasons fit
exactly as if the blackbirds
weren't racing in pairs

on either side of a line,
and the white moths of July
filling the small jar of the air

weren't the one thing you carried
alone into all that snow saying:
Woods are for lovers,

the sun singling you out
among stems poised in their sap,
walking to a welcome

where no bird sings for an answer
as if a song had to touch a song
in perfect time.

The Drinker's Christmas (from a sequence)

Six floors high in an old hotel, you see
The river you, a hero, rode one war.
You could dive to the deepest safety then.
Death was a place that happened only once.

Now days go deep. You ride them in this room,
Captain of four walls you signed to pay for.
You take yourself down like a careful vessel
Past the depth charge of every lived-out year.

Across from your window the steeple clock
Moves in the dark. Every hour hits.
Streetlights come on like harbors
In that time you say has gone by for you.

Rat Poem

On a hot night in mid-November,
I heard them, blood serious,
making arrangements over my head.
I lay in the dark listening
to my place in a house.

I'd always trusted divisions,
believing the dead were safe.
Those rats were so sure of my house,
establishing themselves in structure
as if it were proof.

The Father Maker

Marked by pipes, circled by one neighbor,
your fifteen acres are no farm.
The gate is yours, the right of way
to the line of oaks the deed says
begins your land. Eight months after
you died alone, your only son
and I entered your only kingdom.

In the Texas August, six-inch grass
pricked and buzzed. We watched the herd
a farmer grazes there by contract,
dug up a stiff-rooted bush to plant
on a bank of the water hole you stocked.
That muddy tank can't keep fish,
the farmer says, is too narrow to clear.

Nevertheless, we go back to sink
fresh branches to make green life.
In fall and winter, not much changed.
The frizzled trees shed copper leaves,
looked like old men not grown enough.
The cows were friendlier, had calves
and lost their teeth and looks by spring.

If they're lucky, people don't change.
They clear. This deed is the word
you couldn't speak. Around us are scenes
you didn't describe: the radiant tractor
stopped in sunset, the field where horses
touch in sleep. Your land. Now your son's.
Here seasons are words in the earth.

Sunday Afternoon at White Rock Lake

Across the lake the harbor
was a bundle of ashen sticks.
The trees were still as carvings.
Your father hid in the car
with gin and the Mormon choir
while you and I went walking.

You wanted to sit in the rowboat,
bedded deep in reeds,
the floor an inch in water
but the seats dry enough.
You steered from a bow that swayed
toward its length of hemp rope.

You said we were sailing for joy.
I cleared my head for a poem.
The car on the hill was dark
when finally we got back,
your father asleep at the wheel
over the news and weather

Daughter in Texas

From one fall to another south
Two thousand miles was the move
We had to make. That year the trees
Were strangers: live oak, cottonwood,
Mimosa, redbud, mock orange
With its hard, green fruit, all surface
And fake meat like our change.

For years like an expert mime you
Placed New England a locked house
Around you.   At sixteen, three years
Away, you made a subject of one
Mock orange from the tree in our yard,
Drew knotted lines in pale pencil
As if to touch too hard might break you.

That bumpy rind looked frail as you,
Attentive to its own design.
The next fall you went south
To college. Your drawings darkened,
More accurate than you could bear.
In the year you were to lose a child
You lived without touching anywhere.

You said you had spoiled yourself.
With too much time, with too much place.
For years I saw our mock orange
Huddle its fallen fruit inward
As if still bearing those broken rinds.
I bless your children never born,
The green fruit shaping our hands.

Breakdown with Starlings

That winter every afternoon
the starlings came for bread. They ate,
then flew away in one body.

I watched them from a bedroom window
in a small, rented house. That winter
I didn't throw bread to birds.

No cure can be single and sure
as starlings flying. Every day
that winter my yard was light as bread.

Ouija

No tree like that one blooms anywhere else
I know of. Every other year it showered
white petals on the brick walk to our door.
The suitors came with flowers in their hair
like blessings, foreseen by the one, round eye
of the Ouija board, family friend, ogling
our destinies over our crowding knees.
Most of the time that pointer moved to please,

proving, glib oracle, that what counts
are questions. That eye circled for mates
like targets, reported the day, the month, the year
the war would end. Respectable spook, how
could we doubt your combinations? Your talk
was clearer than a tree, blessing or not.
Out of your sharp-cornered world, your yes and no,
the answers spelled. Only the names came true.

East to Parents (from a sequence)

The sun is coming up like a toy,
brightest ball in the nursery corner.
In the harbor the boats are put away.
The train track winds and shines.
The only one awake in their house,
I watch this sun's small neighborhood
aging to a fresh start.

One of a kind in the family ark
must be quiet as the glass-eyed animals
the children take to bed at night,
magic for the dark, for the dove
back again with no ground for a house.
Make room. The pairs are working in blood.
The sun is crossing its own light.

Thanksgiving House

That sister's was the house we thought of last
for Thanksgiving dinner after her husband
left. He always cooked the turkey and trimmings
and told her what pies to bake for in-laws
who shook his ornament house for their pleasure.

The spring I was her guest overnight, North
after years Southwest, I didn't notice
her sleeping alone in the living room
or the dwarf orange tree in the hall she said
had a breakdown from five children fighting.

And she had no time for the late April
snowfall I rushed outside to see
melt in warm winds, snow dissolving in earth
her husband had turned over for summer,
swirling to nothing in the grey bright air.

Lilacs

On my parents' lawn the lilac trees
Are single, small and frail in beds
Of yellow stone. My father tends them
This cold morning, says he loves spring
For lilacs. I ask him if he remembers
Lilac trees so close they made
A house for children. He nods,
Glad of this image he doesn't fail.

In his seventy-sixth year, my father
Thinks himself into position
Around each tree—his blood walls harden—
He stops to plan the rising of his hand,
Watches its halting route, then waits
To walk till the ground is sure
Of him. In one morning I count
More than a dozen starts in terror.

His voice gone with the morning's work
By noon, he picks a basket of lilacs,
The scent between us on the table
Of a tree house briefly in bloom,
A shelter growing its boundary
In those days of lengthening light,
Voices calling from windows: *Time,
Children, time now to come home.*

Grandmother Singing

The backstairs were a box of light
the morning I heard you sing
in our house, Grandmother, ready
for the Met at twenty-two, caught
by a rich old man of your own choosing.
No bird, you swallowed your voice, medicine
that made you sicker. That loud, bad
digestion embarrassed the whole
family who didn't know music.
Nobody knows why you left the concert
at "Goodbye, my Beloved," weeping,
why I heard you in that walled,
narrow staircase with the window
at one end as if one time were all
in a shaft of a thousand motes blazing.

Garlic

Sure of its medicinal punch,
I'm not scared off by the news story
of the boy who choked in his sleep
and died with garlic in his throat
to ward off vampires.

The ceramic garlic house,
a temple with holes for breathing,
holds a nugget that scours lungs,
loosens the clog in the bloodstream,
terrorizes worms.

Entering my house after a while
elsewhere, the odor of garlic
from a remnant lodged in the wide
throat of the disposal sometimes
embarrasses me

with the truth I've taken garlic
as many have taken lovers
for worse not better. This pungent bud,
purple-veined and green-hearted, hustles
my rank solitude.

The Bakery Sonnet

Sunday afternoons when Mr. Goldman
visits the bakery there's always a crowd.
Everyone takes a number, mills among
the exhibits: round, tan loaves piled like stones,
triangle pastries gaudy as tropical fish,
yellow cakes, halved to show the brown marble.
At his turn, he doesn't deliberate,
points here, there, today (sighing) permits
another, the special, a three-fruit ring,
turns to the ones still waiting, says to them:
Have you noticed everyone here is fat?
A few laugh. Solemn now, he bears the boxed
weight, the scarlet cherry, the gold apricot
to kindle the house where his thin wife waits.

The Street People Refuse the City Shelter

Passing up supper, shower, bed,
they enter the winter night, small
to them now as a place worn thin
at the threshold, bottles held close,
their own names like secret messages
in the wrong hands.
                The oil-drum fire
lights up the heart, the head, the life
lines of cupped hands into itself.
There's light enough. The stars are clear
in this cold, are personal as sleep.

An Elegy Rose

They say Queen Elizabeth feared roses,
and I'm no gardener, though I'm planting a rose,
Father, on your birthday. I've dug through roots
tough as knotted twine.
                              Here April is cold
under a pale sun, the soil is stony,
and there's a wind through these leafless stumps, raw
from the greenhouse, the root in a cardboard box
which must go into the ground with the rose.

There are courtesies in the wildest field
unheard of in a formal garden. Goldenrod,
Queen Anne's lace, the yellow daisy die
without accusation whereas one spot
on a rose leaf condemns a gardener who
remembers your perfect roses.
                              Father, for you
I lower this rose, another transient,
in a box that melts as the root moves out.

Heart

For Joseph Shuman

Remember how it boomed in the walls
of the Hemisfair heart exhibit,
the miles of blood on the screen?
In the hospital emergency room,
the tape bunched and coiled at the machine
like news from the stock exchange.

Now you are fenced in a high bed,
tilted at thirty degrees, hooked up
to the cardiac-unit screen, a live
performance that could go haywire.
All night you are a celebrity.
Even your dreams make waves.

The small black box slaps your back
as you turn over; the plugs suck
at your skin. You won't die alone.
At that Hemisfair in Texas,
South American Indian acrobats
circled high in the air with torches.

That was the year American nuns
shortened their skirts and let out
their faces. Three on our bench watched,
heads thrown far back, those fires go
around a pole higher than anywhere
in San Antonio for the first time.

The Dentist's Walnut Tree

Early for his first job of the day
—my five-day-dying right front tooth—
I study the sun-kindled leaves
yellowing in late October,
of an ancient, half-dead walnut
the narrow, open window frames.

I'm bibbed and drugged and left alone.
From all directions sparrows fly
to the tree's living lower half.
They bounce on thin branches, shake free
more leaves, exit in one rising
over the desolate top limbs.

The dentist comes back. I tell him
I like his tree. He says the tree
needs doctoring but isn't his.
At the joints of his drill's long arm
the discs are spinning. A hook drains
saliva into a whirling bowl.

My mouth is loud as a building site.
I breathe my dust, my tooth calcined
into my elements. The root
sealed, the dentist offers mouthwash.
Behind him, the ailing walnut
looks ready for the next patient.

From

Her BMW and Other Poems (2007)

Day Off in Danville, Virginia

That hot August noon the crew
laying tar stopped their machines
and left us, my daughter on a pass
from the state hospital, and me
picnicking in a city park.

We ate sandwiches from a cooler
—two workers seriously at lunch—
hours away from barred doors,
the bag search at the patient entrance,
the therapists' question: *How to live?*

Our boundaries the mall, the mill store, museum,
we chose that day the museum tour
with a highlight view of the roped-off room
where Jefferson Davis gave up a war,
afterward in the museum shop

came upon such colors in a painting,
a wall-length meadow extravagance,
more accurate than anywhere seen,
that for a moment even in Danville
nothing could work without us.

A Reading

From time to time she would give me
her hand to read: pale lines, pale palm,
like her early pencil drawings,
the still life fruit shy of itself.
That fall after the hospital,
she asked if I saw a difference.

I'm searching, she said of the years
of every loss: work, partner, home,
finally her health. She would wait
all night in her car for the chance
to see the psychic she trusted
to say where good luck might find her.

She doesn't take much time with me.
To look back and see the future
needs no palm reader. Amateur,
I saw no line marked with her choice
for her life in seasons ahead,
the lines as she'd lived them tentative.

Pegasus

With Elizabeth at her window
in cardiac care we could see
the hospital chopper Pegasus
four stories down land with its cargo
of hurt-alive bodies like hers
the night she died, spoke to the dead,

muffled in tubes, bruised with rescue,
attendants at her side, her life
itself conferring distinction
she had no idea of that week
in intensive care, lost to our
signals, and when she could hear us,

she repeated the word *earring*,
somehow knowing the violence
that had brought her back four times from death
had cost her an earring, yet she
couldn't recognize her brother
(thought he was her dentist), couldn't

recall how she made up her eyes
while her screen showed her heart failing
or the two-hour ambulance ride
to another hospital for tests,
her ailment not rare for a woman
her age with her habits, her hardships:

Prinzmetal's Angina or how
she searched for cigarettes, just one
of which, doctors warned, could kill her,
out of bed, trailing connections,
reading over and over what
I wrote explaining her whereabouts

and why. Then finally unhooked
from her guardian machines, in her robe,
she smoked outside the main entrance
the first cigarette of her life
as a sequel to death, familiar
enough to convince her she lived.

Labor Day Sonnet

In the Community Services house,
lent for her recovery with neighbors
James, hearing voices, Tom, bipolar, Dennis
at her door all hours for cigarettes,
his stereo loud as a live concert,
more counselor than patient, out of place
there as her furniture out of storage
after three homeless years, that '94
Labor Day, food stamps spent for a hot dog
cookout, she invited the neighborhood
whose labor was living, their turnout more
than her provisions, her kitchen cupboard
emptied of all but one paprika can,
on a desolate shelf, a gift left over.

Italy

For her birthday dinner she chose
a *ristorante* in downtown
historic America, spoke
to our waiter in Italian
about her dream someday to live
in Italy. Interrupting,
he explained he was Hispanic.

Afterward she bought a pillow,
one side red velvet, the other
a brocade cat, a lucky cat,
she hoped, left behind in her place
homicide police had circled
with crime-scene tape, her door locked then,
windows closed, her life there secured.

Pinwheel

At Sammy T's where we'd had lunch
two months before your burial
tomorrow, watching a pinwheel

in a window across the street
spinning Christmas, recalling how
you said here: "We had a nice time,"

I wonder if you meant just that day
I drove two hours to see you
after a dream, your eyes closed, ivy

on your forehead, sure you'd told me
in your way you wouldn't live long,
or if you summed up all the times

turning us alike toward the world
in consolations short of joy,
new to this town so soon finding

the two pastels we would go back
over and over to see if
still for sale in the shop window,

agreeing to ask the artist
to hold them for us. Together
we could pay for them by Christmas.

Her BMW

Elizabeth Herrington (1948-1994)

The mechanic who bought her '83
BMW has promised to make
those repairs she intended: peeling paint
sanded, dents hammered out, body restored
to its original dark blue, leaks sealed,
tattered insides, smoky as a tavern,
and the broken right side-view mirror replaced,
its history since she'd owned it disappeared.

In six years, 100,000 miles driven
from one home lost to another, the car
ran on minimal attention, broke down
only in sight of help and cash, a roof
any night at the side of the road,
once almost her heart-attack deathbed, parked
at a 7-Eleven. A store clerk,
two paramedics happening by, saved her life.

Deliverance car: down a mountain's edge
in sheet rain, on the road east she followed west,
luxury other homeless couldn't forgive,
an address in itself, her very home,
that November night in the lot outside
her apartment where she lay murdered
—her killer unknown—and just this mileage
to tell exactly how far she had come.

Peach Orchard (from a sequence)

Following signs, we came to no
orchard, no acres of peach trees,

but a stand with peaches for sale,
a patch of close-planted peach trees.

We sat under a canopy.
I ate frozen yogurt (peach,

of course). You lighted a cigarette,
forbidden since your heart attack,

tired of peaches in season,
that rumor of a real orchard.

Clothing the Dead

Late summer racks of merchandise
on the mall sidewalk, marked down,
catch me on my way somewhere else,
not wanting to single her out
from among those fabric shoulders,
no longer here for the white blouse
she might have grabbed for the bargain.
Impossible not to see her
in the blue-green jumper—arms
thin from meals postponed past hunger,
fingers waving a cigarette—
appraising with me this window
of mannequins dressed for the fall,
a new season, a change of clothes.

Perfume

Whenever her favorite perfume
went on sale, I'd buy a supply

the way I'd stock up on candles
or toilet paper, not luxuries.

Je Reviens, White Shoulders, L'Aimant:
she moved in air identified,

solidarity in a scent
with the world's fragile offerings.

On our last shopping trip, she chose
a bottle of something nameless,

cheap, brightly colored, from a bin,
bargain enough, though not her kind,

that too strong, too sweet scent urgent
for notice apart from her.

Benches

Placed-for–the view benches
on the condominium grounds
seat no one most of the time,

empty for the after-work
tennis match on the lighted court,
for the stream where the surface moves

with circles of unseen life,
passed up by runners, walkers
for health like me, this morning

inviting my daughter, in life,
lover of intervals benches
provide. Losing her eyeglasses

somewhere she couldn't remember,
she stopped searching, sure of their loss,
found them on her bench with a view.

Namesake

The leaves of the geranium I named
for her are curled up like her hands
the night of her heart attack, a sign,
the nurse said, she was giving up.
But she let death go that time.

So this geranium, four years ago
all leaves when I invoked
her spirit on its behalf, scared
if nothing changed, eternity
might also have its boundaries,

shortly flowered in such abundance
friends noticed. Now these stiffened stems
look past treatment as usual,
at risk to prove her here in a flower,
performing for joy in the world.

Virginia Center for the Creative Arts, 2000

I *Trains*

Fields here are the color
and height I remember
from years ago,
this morning early
after rain
each curving blade
beaded alike,

tracks in the gully
(the double track
becoming one
at the signal light)
still active with trains
I run to the bridge
to catch underneath

and make a wish,
this time for words
exact as a shower
overnight on a field
for a daughter's lifelong
losses she met
in a word: *setback.*

And just that word
to cover her absence,
her death no more
than a train's wait
for a track to clear,
this trail of words
a caboose waving?

II *Sylvia Moves Out*

A friend since the afternoon
I met her unloading branches
for her sculptures, vine balls
in sizes various as planets,
packed up now in her truck bed,
Sylvia says she'll write, wants to hear
more about my child murdered,

whose spirit revived a geranium.
who could find me anywhere,
who would grow plants in corners
of rooms like this studio
with its smell of a fresh paint
future as if there were no
such thing as temporary.

III *Woodchuck*

At dinner someone mentions a sighting,
a resident appearing too often
to discredit, not familiar, bigger
than a rat, chestnut-brown, and slow moving.
City folk, most of us, we guess. *Hedgehog?*
Groundhog? Finally *woodchuck* satisfies.

So I'm prepared several days later
for the stir in the field near my door,
the body lumbering through sunlit brush,
a celebrity to transients, surprised
by a creature requiring no other
than ground-level horizons, at home here.

If You Were Egyptian

If instead of ashes
in a twentieth-century urn,

you were Egyptian
in the time of pharaohs,

you might turn up
in a resin mask,

discoveries unwound
in your many wrappings:

a brass ashtray,
copper skillet,

a miniature vase
of blue pottery,

that one belonging
you never let go:

the matriarch icon,
her body a household,

candle in a jar,
your face in firelight

at the small hearth
of its flame, you

here in the witness,
the secrecy of things.

From

Open Season (2015)

Visit to Jan in Open Season

Enon Valley, Pennsylvania

All the first evening her five dogs barked outside
as if I were a danger in the house
of my friend, a poet, not a farmer,
newcomer to her acres of farmland
under light snow after the long fall drought,

muddying our path through her deer-tracked woods
to a stone shell, cellar of her house torched
by someone the neighbors know but won't name,
both in red hats to keep from getting shot
also on her farm, a children's story:

nine horses, a white duck, two fat-necked geese,
the rooster who froze in a tree and thawed alive,
famous for his night with a skunk in his cage,
the dogs quiet when we left in her truck
for the Amish blacksmith's, along the road

trailer homes, in a gray-lit Amish yard
a clothesline of blue and purple dresses,
winter wheat green-alive in whitened fields
and footprints crossing, telling the hardship
of distance, losing hold in the warming wind.

Old, My Father Invented a Machine

Old, my father invented a machine
to print cloth when he'd lost
to a brand-name conglomerate his small
south Massachusetts mill.

Once I toured his mill, saw patterned fabrics
rise overhead on belts
to a jigging racket and stink of dye,
heard him above the noise

explain how the big boys had bought him out,
but he had a new plan
to make us rich. Afterwards in a room
hung with tools and photos

of stages in the mill's long life, he showed me
his scratchings on paper,
embryo of a machine that could print
more cloth in less time.

In the one-lamp glare on his drawing board
he imagined wheels, gears,
and doctor blades which snarled and failed,
and finally worked the dream

that made his backer rich, my father poor.
He never spoke again
of his namesake, housed in a Southern state,
efficient in glory

and practical cloth. I have a sample
of its first fruit, a length
of pink roses on white cotton, cut clean
from that victory run.

A Family Chair

Sent to me, its inheritor,
the eighteenth-century maple chair
emerges from a five-foot carton
more character than furniture:
the grip of downward-curving arms,
the slightly forward-tilting posture

from metal treads on the back legs,
inclining the chair's occupant
toward family clamor, mine, the day
I asked my father what he lived for,
and as if in the chair he could give
no other answer, he said, "My children."

I once heard in a museum
a Congo people's funeral trumpets,
wooden horns as family icons
to encourage their dead's contented presence.
This chair in its seated silence
makes room for my own to enter.

Courtship

The moon is a smudge of light
over the uneven dark
horizon from end to end
of the small, framed oil painting.

The tree in the right foreground,
unleafing or about to leaf,
inclines toward the moon halfway
up or down the sky as if

to clarify a neutral moment
the moon might yield its way,
no colors but shades
of beige and gray in this work

of a painter later known
for his New England landscapes
inscribed to my mother
with the date above his name,

a birthday and courtship gift
she hung for sixty-eight years
after she said no, after
August 11, 1917.

The Size of Childhood

Bored with safety, sometimes we'd cross
acres of tall grass to a house
unlocked and vacant, sunlight an echo
in rooms with yellow walls, empty
except for a trunk-size box
of fusty-smelling costumes, laid
to rest like the one who wore them:
Richard Mansfield, his fame unknown
to children claiming for ourselves
an abandoned cottage, a tomb for clothes
without bones to rise and accuse
—those outfits in rigid repose,
seen once and not disturbed again—
nor did his widow, old lady
now and then sighted on her cane-paced walks,
interrupt us, leaving each time
what we'd find returning, rooms cleared
of evidence, air no one breathed,
the resident wardrobe not moved.

Lighthouse Watch

Daylight disclosed the distance the lighthouse
light brought near: three whites and a red
I could see from my pillow, signaling me
—awake late on a summer night—
to the window one more time in the spell
of its rhythm like a dance step to join,
not missing a beat, no land, no water
between us, that unhindered darkness
I had to make sure of again
and again, afraid I'd get caught
out of bed, a child not in place
in a house so quiet I once heard
pages of a book open on the floor
riffled by a breeze from nowhere.

Arthur, a Memoir

Afterwards two friends called
with chicken soup. They spoke
of the deaths of their elderly pets
by euthanasia. I described
my sudden decision at the sight

of that much blood from tumors
inoperable from the start.
I mentioned the strange cough
since summer, the arthritis,
the epilepsy, the heart murmur.

But the day Arthur died,
he walked around the lake,
stopping as usual
for deep investigations,
making himself a stone

as I tried to pull on, and ate
with gusto the slice of pizza
I baked for his last meal
and had a happy expression
looking over my shoulder

in the car and didn't object
to the vet's table but sat
expectantly as if he agreed.
The first needle didn't work.
At the second, he cried out,

in his eyes a look. He knew.
His weight in my arms,
I heard a sound in his throat.
The vet placed the stethoscope.
"He's gone," he said.

So much like a person,
friends would say. The way
I talked about him
at work some people thought
a beagle was my husband.

He slept in my bed,
preferred vegetables and Mozart.
He might have died in his sleep
naturally as we all wish,
companion to his secret pain.

Opera Heart

Alone with the set I listen
to the live-on-TV audience
scuttling coughs for the curtain rise
on the Met stage, there with you once

on an overdue honeymoon
at the Saturday matinee,
dressed in our best—a lady
asking if we were from the west—

for Verdi's *Don Carlos,* captives
bound to the beat of the auto-da-fé,
heart-stir for our own duet
to outlast error on a grand scale.

Years without you tonight a nun,
Puccini's *Suor Angelica,*
her madness forgiven, taken
to Heaven, could bring the house down.

Overnight

The train coach lights go out.
Strangers sleep side by side
as in a giant nursery,

while cities cross faces
like flashlights checking.
Low to the earth the moon

races backwards. I sleep,
wake up to the shine
of rain on the window,

the station unannounced,
a hushed exodus
from the nighttime household.

Pumpkin Judging

For Nathaniel

The children came with pumpkins to carve
before dark and the judging, each child
alone with a knife and the deadline dark
and a pumpkin who could be anyone.

Even the late ones finished in time
for the performance, the house lights off,
the better to see the assembly
crossing the black lawn. What could we make

of twenty-six candlelit faces,
all personalities, none alike?
Whatever the style of mouth and eyes,
holes or slits or crescents, whatever

patterns on cheeks, on chins, on foreheads,
whatever adorned the pumpkin flesh
(a pepper tongue, a pirate's nose ring
and every kind of hat), we judges

couldn't agree on best or worst,
judged the winner joined twin pumpkins
with no ornament to distract us
from its two-headed, double gaze.

A Postcard from Spain

For R.B.H. (1920-1974)

This postcard survived a box of letters
kept too long in a damp cellar, postmarked
29 July '68, the scene
(named in the top, left-hand corner above
your *Dearest*): Toledo, a partial view,
a white-foamed river, a narrow shore, a pool
mirroring a stone house, a zigzag road
uphill in rock past bulwark walls to dark
green groves, milky-blue sky, the palace where
you wrote you went because it was Sunday.

I don't remember the card or the trip
when you still signed openly to the world
All my love. The address tells me we lived
then in our last house, a pomegranate tree
in the yard and at our bedroom window
the gardenia bush of florist-perfect blooms.
One night you brought home a guest, a stranger
from the North, lighted the driveway for him
to see the gardenia bush in flower.
You filled at least a dozen plastic bags,

shaking water over the limp petals.
Hands full, he left us, astonished at joy
so suddenly in that house. Past divorce,
your death, why does that moment seem sent now
as this postcard once, specific as your
news of the weather in Spain: *like Texas
but drier and without air-conditioning?*
The spires on the palace turrets thin out
to needle points in the sunlit, clear air.
I wonder how far you walked in that heat.

Not Quite Loneliness in Texas

Three months here in a rented house
where former tenants left only
nail holes in doors and papered walls
and one his name on the mailbox:
Fabergé, I watch a backyard,
winter bleached, bird shadows crossing.

The blue jays, the finches make plans,
not wishes; a jay hammers the ground,
finches change places on a branch,
indifferent to past occupants.
Fabergé's name has outlasted
two rounds of tenants. He lived alone,

died somewhere in these rooms. Shy, proud
of his name (not the perfume company,
the landlord says he emphasized),
descendant of artists to the Tsar,
professor, famous in his own right,
he talked to himself in Russian.

Inventor of an apparatus
for clocking traffic in a beehive,
a scale to weigh butterfly wings,
year after year he burned dinners
on our terrible stove while birds
seized and let go an empty yard.

Facing Fort Trumbull with Charles

Never used as a fort, Charles tells me
in his car parked in the visitors' lot
of the state park, newly developed

at a cost of millions and neighborhoods.
He jokes that grass on the fort's roof
was for catching cannon balls, speaks

of the war he knows, artillery
in the Battle of the Bulge: *War
is to lose people, that's what it's for.*

May sunlight like a color wash
calls attention to the fort's façade,
the darkness behind symmetrical

lookout slits in stone Charles praises,
seen rarely before its present use,
featured with lamps, a winding walk,

a river view for the future hotel,
occupants at their windows to watch
traffic in season at the going cost.

Between the Worshippers and the Deer

For Philip

One rainy Sunday morning in June
just past a church, parking lot full,
ahead of me a deer, full grown,

crossed a sloping lawn and the road
into the woods. Seconds later its twin
in size followed, my small car right

after over the two-lane asphalt,
the foliage shaken where they'd gone
on the trail of some known, seasonal meal.

Eternal Sleep

In Maureen McCabe's *Eternal Sleep,*
an 8 x 14 box montage,
the swirling shapes in black and gray

—a photo of an angel sculpture
and one of a woman outstretched,
head fallen back, interwoven—

recall the pattern on the walls
of the passage grave on Hag's Hill
in Ireland where I watched her

lay sheets of paper over the stone
to rub to life. In this piece, a break
in the overall design shows

a young girl's face, her eyes closed,
a pink rose in her yellow hair
and three at her throat as if just placed there

like the spiral figures she brought forth
in that burial chamber cell
for the company in eternal sleep.

New Poems

Crossing

At this time of year a pair
of windows where I live— cleared
of the crepe myrtle's season—
includes a sky-traffic view.

On my watch a flight across
one I look to see enter
the other as if the plane
requires my attention.

Daughter Waking

In the hospital her short-term memory
tested daily, she remembered
the doctor who waited by her bed

every morning for her to wake up,
one of the team in the cardiac unit
admitting her the night the ambulance

brought her from another hospital,
her eyes I saw with what knowledge
on them as she answered their questions,

opened from her four-minute death,
that glimpse she mentioned of her father
lost to a heart attack years before.

Discharged, her body a celebrity
like a skater's in that winter's Olympics
she watched on the shelter TV,

at a table of paperwork—
her rescue's reckoning—she said:
"I lay back and died, and now I have this."

The child in Mark's Gospel story,
raised from the dead, her parents told:
Give her something to eat.

Among the Absent

Overstayed among the absent,
in the first month of the year
I encounter Canada geese,

trespassers like me on the grounds
of a high-rise residence complex,
boundary of a wildlife preserve,

more than a hundred so it looks,
crowding the lawn between a marsh
and windows to a nine-story height,

with stately gait clearing the walk
for me at their stopover feast
stepping carefully in our discourse.

Dining with Marjorie

Each with her poems in a gloved hand,
we enter a Chinese restaurant,
take a table under a strong light,
order, exchange our poems and read.

A few pages in, I look up
to see her face losing its expression
as she reads poems—like hers—lifelines
to the men we haven't let go:

the suicidal father dies
of cancer, the drinker's heart
gives out, the much younger lover
becomes a friend.
                     But here's a fish,

whole, with a stiff crust in red sauce.
Marjorie rakes the ribs, shows me
where to cut for meat. Her chopsticks
flare and snap with grace. I work hard

with a fork and spoon, avoiding the glazed
and rooted eye.
                    Two fortune cookies
end our meal. Her hand decides.
"You will succeed in work," is mine

and hers: "Eat and be happy."
She laughs. "I could so easily
have gotten yours," she says, the fish,
borne off, down to its thorny spine.

Room

Hospitable no matter the place,
shelter, hospital, section eight,
in the psychiatric ward's cage of smoke.
hostess of the visitors' lounge,
she presented her fellow patient,
a woman broken by disregard.

Introducing me to her room,
her home in a year of rooms,
the bureau missing a drawer,
the cot-size mattress, the street
in the window without a shade,
she included in her courtesy.

William Meredith at the Library of Congress

...and the worst
That can be said of any one of us:
He didn't pay attention.

William Meredith
"Fables about Error"

Dressed for the reading that night
in velvet jackets, mine brand new,
we met outside the entrance,

Consultant in Poetry,
his student years past
in a class sometimes held

in his house by a Connecticut river.
Too hot inside, he mentioned,
for his jacket, my thought too,

body heat to do no harm,
what I would hear him say
he wished for his teaching.

To find a good seat
in the hall, I couldn't linger
with him in the portico,

paying attention to temperature,
the air mild for the season,
cool enough for a jacket.

On the Railway Bridge

The light snowfall a benediction
for my early evening walk,

on the railway bridge I made a wish,
train thunder underneath.

In the shaken air I heard my voice:
Make me whatever you will,

the short freight on its way out of sight
at the curve far down the track,

with regret then for my game turned prayer
in just that oncoming snow.

Mad in the Blue Ridge

Stranger in a mountain city,
chosen for economic reasons,
I had for company a voice

I'd once turned to books to silence.
One from that time I reopened:
Burton's *Anatomy of Melancholy*,

his seventeenth-century mad
with me in the kindred torment
of a head I couldn't get right.

Finally at a Blue Ridge height,
I gripped rock in a handhold climb
for a view with room for demons.

Pilgrim Climb

I'll go alone, I announced
to companions on a trip to Ireland,
not wanting tourist chitchat
on a sacred mountain climb.
Allowed two hours,

I circled Saint Patrick's statue
the required seven times,
picked my way up a slope,
pilgrims sprinting past me,
paused for a man in descent,

not young, in a tailored suit.
I asked did he find it hard.
To be sure, the last part,
wouldn't try it in *those shoes*
without a staff and, yes,

on the past Sunday's pilgrimage,
A little girl went over.
It happens sometimes.
Onward I met a woman
with two boys: *Their first time up!*

One gave me his wooden plank,
needed nearer the top.
Crouched to a child-size staff,
leaning away from the edge
in the hush of increasing height,

trembling, I shifted my view,
no one in sight to remark
my sandals gripping downward
to near where the path began,
in a level grass hideaway

to wait out my given time
in doubt of what tale to tell
to prove some Irish wonder,
on my soles Croagh Patrick grit,
dust itself a relic.

Moira Baking

Moira Banks-Dobson, 1987-2012

Her homework the Book of Job
the birthday we baked a cake,
she asked what I made of suffering
so little understood.

Knowing she fought depression,
I sent her Les Murray's book
Killing the Black Dog.
She wrote: "We all suffer."

In her mother's kitchen
how carefully she measured,
no yolk in the egg whites beaten
to fold in the batter last.

Virginia Storm, 2003

Firemen at my door warning me to leave,
I drove that night to my sister's
for our second hurricane
under one roof.

In our Connecticut home
at a window, candles in our hands,
we saw on the far horizon
our town on fire,

the next day walked neighborhood grounds
in a searchlight sun on everywhere gone,
the beach with a crowd of hundreds
to witness the waves.

In the gray morning's motionless quiet,
I followed her clearing her yard,
two in procession with branches
light enough for our years.

Mammon, the Collector's Daughter

N.P.J., 1902-1992

No stranger robbed her, a widow
alone, doors left unlocked in case
of fire or a fall the crew
from Emergency could reach her,
safe awhile in her treasure house,
surviving weekends on teacups of scotch.

At eighty-two, a resident
four months of a nursing home, she
signed away treasures in storage,
furniture from her father's house
a magazine named one of twelve
of America's most beautiful.

Near ninety, near death, she would dream
at her room's one window, curtains
removed for light, a view of shrubs,
a small maple, the bird feeder
to attract company for the hours
between trays of impossible food.

In shabby shoes, her teeth let go,
she remembered a punishment
she liked as a child, to be shut
in the mansion linen closet,
for whatever her mischief
doing time where she pleased.

Dogwood

White dogwood his preference
in trees flowered in time

for our walks on the grounds
of the school where we taught,

I attached to another,
he much younger, bipolar,

in his tiny car hurtled
over snowfield roads,

in a winter-beached rowboat
one night on a country lake,

moment by moment afloat
on water that cold, that deep.

Grinder

For Anne

After my sister's burial
I walked with my first born that night
in a town once our home.

She wanted a grinder. At the shop
we found she told our waiter how
to make the one she remembered

for her order to go
swaddled in the December cold
through streets we had left behind.

Fire Drill at Pequot Day

For fire drill at my first school—
three rooms above a parking garage—
we climbed out a classroom window,
shepherded by the principal,
a pioneer in the learning field,
the sill let go for the top rung
of a ladder two stories to the ground,
our exit the upper grades room,
desks painted rainbow colors,
in her unlocked desk answer books
we sneaked to copy. Finding out,
she heard confessions in the bathroom,
on the toilet seat absolved our betrayal
of a space she trusted us to hold.

What Singer

Basic Musicianship class over
someone asked our professor—
voice teacher in her last year
before retirement—what singer
alive in her lifetime she judged best.

She took a step back from her desk,
holding the room for her choice.
A young man, she told us, *homeless,*
at this campus on a scholarship.
He dropped out, came back, left again.
what happened to him never learned.

Expecting a name to recognize,
in her silence we stayed at attention
for that voice in her hearing known.

Descent through Rocks to Water

A descent through rocks to water
my daughter and I put off
for an earlier start, light to last,
a memory postponed of a hike
like others to map the Blue Ridge,
once scared from a hooded green thicket
by a quiet too near our own.
The afternoon she committed herself
to the state hospital she asked me
to go with her on a late-day climb
before she left, and I refused,
smarting from our recent quarrel,
too certain then of a mountain
to learn, trails for us to resume.

Loughcrew, 1982

Halfway to the passage grave
I sat down with Charles in high grass,
the others in our party
ahead on the burial mound,
around us verdant farmland
like the countryside at Newgrange
he proclaimed could be Vermont,
not Ireland in my snapshots.
Continuing our approach,
we heard voices from the tomb,
a rush of wind to meet us,
crouching for lintel stone
to crawl through earth to the cell
for burning megalith bones.

The Eagle's Nest

Christmas, 1974

In the room you named the eagle's nest
on your bed at least two days,
the landlord guessed, I looked for you
to take up your life where you left off:

the AA handbook—your name inscribed—
in a chair, on the desk the Big Book,
photos of your parents, our son,
the corncob pipe with fresh tobacco,

in a side drawer bundled and tied,
our letters from your years at sea,
hardly enough space on the walls
for your achievements in their black frames,

near as the phone our distance,
a call for me to turn on TV,
the Mormon Tabernacle Choir
momentarily in performance.

Alongside Woods

Winter nights
in bed by a window
alongside woods,
I listened to ice
crack on branches

of trees I could place,
the maple leaf
I sent to you where
redbud blooms
in February,

reminder of years
by other woods,
lights out for the night
before we slept
to hear how near.

Starting Over

Far southwest of a northeast left
for a better paid future in Texas,

that first fall after a day of rain
we woke to an overnight freeze,

garden beds ice brimmed,
cars creeping as if learning the world.

The daughter, twelve, who refused to join
her sister, father and me on drives

to get to know Texas better,
shutting herself in her room, shades down,

put on her ice skates for a photo
on a frozen puddle, at home on ice.

Neva Herrington was born and raised in New London, Connecticut. A graduate of Ashley Hall in Charleston, South Carolina, she attended Connecticut College and received the B.A. and M.A. in English from Southern Methodist University. She taught there on a Fellowship and at the Williams School in Connecticut. On the English faculty at Northern Virginia Community College, after retirement she was an adjunct writing instructor at Sweet Briar and Randolph College in Virginia and at St. Edward's University in Texas. She has published three books of poems *Blue Stone* (Still Point Press, 1986), the chapbook *Her BMW* (Pudding House Publications, 2007), and *Open Season* (David Robert Books, 2015). Her poetry has appeared in a number of journals and in the anthologies *Entering the Real World* (Wavertree Press) and *The Anthology of Magazine Verse & Yearbook of American Poetry*. She has also published short fiction. She has been a Fellow at Yaddo and at the Virginia Center for the Creative Arts. She lives in Williamsburg, Virginia.